D1477194

Stages 15 to 16

Y6 / P7

Comprehension

PUPILS' BOOK

Catherine Baker
and Charlotte Raby

ST. MARGARETS PRIMARY SCHOOL
WOODMILL ROAD
DUNFERMLINE KY11 4DQ

OXFORD
UNIVERSITY PRESS

OXFORD
UNIVERSITY PRESS

Great Clarendon Street, Oxford OX2 6DP

Oxford University Press is a department of the University of Oxford.
It furthers the University's objective of excellence in research, scholarship,
and education by publishing worldwide in

Oxford New York

Auckland Cape Town Dar es Salaam Hong Kong Karachi
Kuala Lumpur Madrid Melbourne Mexico City Nairobi
New Delhi Shanghai Taipei Toronto

With offices in

Argentina Austria Brazil Chile Czech Republic France Greece
Guatemala Hungary Italy Japan Poland Portugal Singapore
South Korea Switzerland Thailand Turkey Ukraine Vietnam

Oxford is a registered trade mark of Oxford University Press
in the UK and in certain other countries

© Oxford University Press 2008

Extracts and activities compiled by Catherine Baker

The moral rights of the authors have been asserted

Database right Oxford University Press (maker)

British Library Cataloguing in Publication Data

Data available

ISBN: 978-0-19-846748-9

5 7 9 10 8 6 4

Printed in China by Imago

Acknowledgements

The copyright for each extract is held by the Author, unless otherwise stated. Extracts (in order of appearance): 'Animals in Danger' from *Animals and Us* by Claire Llewellyn, TreeTops Non-Fiction Stage 14; *The Night of the Ticklers* by Paul Shipton, TreeTops Fiction Stage 14; *Climbing in the Dark* by Nick Warburton, TreeTops Playscripts Stage 14; 'The Greek Gods' from *The Greeks* by Mark McArthur-Christie, Oxford Connections; *Never Wash Your Hair* by Margaret McAllister, TreeTops Fiction Stage 14 More Stories A; *Air Raid!* by Jean May, TreeTops Fiction Stage 14 More Stories A; *Antarctic Adventure* by Anna Perera, TreeTops True Stories Stage 14; 'The Moonlit Stream' © James Reeves from *Complete Poems for Children* (Heinemann), reprinted by permission of the James Reeves Estate; *The Worst Team in the World* by Alan MacDonald, TreeTops Fiction Stage 15; 'Robots: Difficult and Dangerous Work' from *Robots – Friend or Foe?* by Sarah Fleming, TreeTops Non-Fiction Stage 15, © OUP; *Trapped!* by Malachy Doyle, TreeTops Fiction Stage 14 More Stories A; 'Alabama' by Khe-Tha-A-Hi from *The Moonlit Stream and Other Poems*, Oxford Literacy Web; *Tomahawk Beckwourth* by Michael Cox, TreeTops True Stories Stage 15; *The Powder Monkey* by Maureen Rylance, TreeTops Fiction Stage 15; 'Triremes' from *The Greeks* by Mark McArthur-Christie, Oxford Connections; *One Girl School* by Jon Blake, TreeTops Fiction Stage 16 More Stories A; 'Westward! Westward!' by H W Longfellow from *The Moonlit Stream and Other Poems*, Oxford Literacy Web; *Macbeth* adapted by Jon Blake, TreeTops Classics Stage 16; 'Fireworks' from *Explosions* by Becca Heddle, TreeTops Non-Fiction Stage 16; 'Greek Battles' from *The Greeks* by Mark McArthur-Christie, Oxford Connections.

The publisher would like to thank the following for permission to reproduce photographs: **p6** NHPA/Martin Harvey, **p7**t NHPA/Joe Blossom, **p7**b NHPA/ Daniel Heuchlin; **p25** Royal Geographic Society/Ranulph Fiennes; **p43** Getty Images/Hulton Archive; **p60** Kimbolton Fireworks.

Cover photograph: OUP

Illustrations: **pp9, 10** Judy Brown; **pp12, 13, 14, 55, 56** Martin Cottam; **pp16, 17, 62** Martin Aston; **pp20, 21** Tim Archibold; **p23** Kenny McKendry; **p26** Trevor Parkin; **pp28, 29** Esther Connon; **p31** John Eastwood; **p34**t Getty/National Geographic, **p34**b Corbis/Reuters, **p35**t Corbis/Roger Ressmeyer, **p35**b Redzone; **pp37, 38** Jane Cope; **pp40, 41** Rachel Pearce; **p45** Robin Lawrie; **p47** Bill Donohue; **p50** Tony Ross; **p53** Stephen Gulbis; **p58**t Gary Swift, **p58**b Martin Cottam; **p59** Matt Buckley; **p63** Chris Brown.

Although every effort has been made to contact the owners of copyright material, a few have been impossible to trace. However, if they contact the Publisher, correct acknowledgement will be made in future editions.

Design by PDQ Digital Media Solutions Ltd

Paper used in the production of this book is a natural, recyclable product made from wood grown in sustainable forests.
The manufacturing process conforms to the environmental regulations of the country of origin.

Note to teachers
The texts in this book are differentiated for use with pupils of different reading abilities.
⟳ easiest text, ⟳⟳ medium text, ⟳⟳⟳ most difficult text

Contents

Introduction

Comprehension Power

Do you know the saying, 'Knowledge is power'? It's certainly true that the more you know and understand, the more opportunities and choices you have. That's one reason why it's worth practising your comprehension skills – they will help you to understand and get the most out of any piece of text that you read. So by using the comprehension strategies below, you can really boost your comprehension power!

Predicting

- When you look at a new piece of text, you get lots of clues from features such as the title, headings, pictures and diagrams and so you can probably work out quite quickly what the text is about. But there are also clues in the smaller details of a text, such as the way one paragraph links into another. These smaller clues can help you deepen your understanding of the text.

- You can use prediction to help you understand how texts are structured. When you've finished reading one paragraph or section, you can predict what the next one will be about.

- Sometimes authors like to surprise readers by challenging our expectations and doing something we don't expect. Comparing what happens in a text with what you thought would happen can be a good way of checking your understanding as you go along.

Imagining

- Many good readers see pictures in their head as they read – pictures of the characters in a story, or a scene from a play or poem, or a description in a non-fiction text.

- Building up these pictures in your head can help you to understand the text.

- Imagining yourself into the text can help you build up a clear picture of it. What would you see, feel, hear etc., if you were there?

- As you read on, you can add to the picture you have of the text – and sometimes you will find that you have to change the picture as you read!
- You can also use drawing, or drama techniques such as role-play and hot-seating, to help you imagine the text.

Questioning & clarifying

- Even very experienced adult readers have lots of questions in their heads as they read a text. In fact, the more experienced the reader, the more likely they are to ask questions as they read! Thinking about your questions helps you to understand the text.
- When you are reading fiction, you can ask questions about why the characters feel or behave the way they do. How does the author decide what will happen next? How does the way characters act influence what happens in the story? Why did the author choose to use particular words, or to tell us about a particular event?
- When you are reading non-fiction, asking lots of questions helps you to understand the text and make links between different parts of the text. It also helps you make links with what you already know about the subject.
- Use the 'look-back' strategy to help you answer your questions by looking back in the text for the answers. You can also use what you already know about the subject – or your own imagination – to answer your questions.
- It can help to keep a note of your questions and come back to them later, or talk about them with someone else who has read the text.

Summarising

- Summarising helps you focus on the most important information in the text.
- When you read fiction, summarising can help you retell the story, write a book review or a blurb, or give reasons when you recommend a book.
- When you read non-fiction, summarising can help you work out the main point of the text, and how the different parts of the text work together.
- Summarising can also help you sum up the author's style, their intention in writing the text, the way the text is put together, etc.

Predicting

Give yourself 10 seconds to look at
this text. What kind of information
do you think it will contain?

Animals in danger

As the human population grows, wild animals and humans are squeezed
closer together. In many parts of the world, animals' natural habitats are
being cleared to make room for building or farming. Some kinds of animals
can adapt to these changes and live side-by-side with people. But most of
them face problems. They do not have enough space to live. They cannot
find enough food. These problems mean fewer and fewer of them survive.
The animals on these pages are all endangered. Could they become extinct?

Endangered!

Name: Goliath frog

Habitat: fast-flowing
rainforest rivers

Distribution:
equatorial Africa

Problems: habitat loss
due to logging,
farming and the
building of dams.
Hunted for food and
the pet trade

Endangered!

Name: Mountain gorilla

Habitat: tropical cloud forests

Distribution: central Africa

Problems: forest habitat has been cleared for timber and to make way for farms, mines and roads

Endangered!

Name: Kakapo

Habitat: forest and scrubland

Distribution: islands off New Zealand

Problems: hunted almost to the point of extinction by dogs, cats, rats and other predators introduced by human settlers

Animals in Danger

Partner activities

I can ...

- use evidence from a text to help me put together a persuasive argument
- comment constructively on my partner's argument

1. Pick one of the animals in the text. Make notes on how it is endangered, the role of humans in endangering it, and what humans could do about it.

2. Use your notes to plan a short persuasive speech explaining what the problem is and why you think people should act to save your chosen animal. Take turns with your partner to try persuading each other.

3. Comment on your partner's speech. What did you like about it? How could they make it more persuasive?

Predicting

Most of the text is in note form, so think carefully about what it is telling you.

Think and write

1. What does the word 'habitat' mean in this text?

2. What problems might animals have if their habitats are destroyed?

3. Which of the three animals mentioned in the text doesn't come from Africa?

4. Why might more animals become endangered as the human population grows?

5. What are human beings doing to cause the Goliath frog to become endangered? Find two things.

6. What kind of place does the Kakapo like to live in?

7. What kind of creature do you think the Kakapo is?

8. What have humans done that has made life difficult for the Kakapo?

9. Do you think that people meant to make life difficult for the Mountain gorilla? Explain why, or why not.

10. What do you think the purpose of this text is? Explain why you think this, and suggest one thing the author could do to make the text more effective.

THE NIGHT OF THE TICKLERS

Imagining

As you read, try to picture what is happening. What would the scene in the radio studio look like? What do the aliens look like?

We started cycling out of the village. My legs ached, but I ignored the pain and forced them to go faster. It felt good to leave all the sound of laughter behind us. Now if we could just make it to the next village and get help…

'Look!' shouted Katy.

A car was parked in the middle of the road. Its lights were on and the driver's door was open. As we got closer we could hear a voice, but when we got there we realized it was coming from the radio. The car was empty. It was our local radio station. The song began and I was about to click the radio off when the DJ interrupted the music.

> This is a news flash. Reports are coming in to the station from people who claim to have seen UFOs – Unidentified Flying Objects. Details are not yet known, but it seems that contact has been made with an alien life form. One eyewitness says that she saw two aliens come out from a silver ball. They then began to tickle people… TICKLE PEOPLE? Is this some kind of joke? It's not April the First, is it?

The DJ did not believe what he was reading. Katy and I just looked at each other. We knew it was no joke.

Suddenly there was a clattering noise on the radio – as if something had been knocked over. It was followed by another sound, one that we knew already: *heh, heh, heh.* A new note of panic appeared in the DJ's voice.

What's going on? Who's there? Wha– ladies and gentlemen, this is incredible! An alien has just made its way into the studio here at Radio Wow FM. I repeat, there is a creature from another world here in the studio with me. It's smiling, it looks friendly. It's moving towards me now, it's reaching its arms out. I think it wants to make contact. I – oo, hey, don't do that! I'm ticklish – hahaha, no, heeheehee, hooooo –

sssssssssssssssssssss

The radio went dead.

The Night of the Ticklers

Partner activities

I can ...

- read a story and predict what might happen next
- write a diary entry from the point of view of one of the characters

1. Discuss with your partner what might happen next in the story. Use your imaginations, but your ideas need to fit in with the story so far!

2. When you have decided what happens next, write a diary entry from the point of view of one of the two children in the story, or of the alien. Your diary entry should explain what happened in the text and what happened next.

Predicting

Use clues from the text to help you think about what might happen next. What is the mood of the story? What do the characters think will happen?

Think and write

1. What are Mike (the narrator) and Katy doing at the start of this text, and why do you think they are doing this?

2. What is strange about the car that Mike and Katy find?

3. Why do you think the car was left like this?

4. What is the name of the radio station that is playing on the car radio?

5. Why does the DJ interrupt the music?

6. Why does the DJ think the story about aliens is a joke?

7. How do you think Mike and Katy know the story about aliens is not a joke? Find two quotes from the text that help you make up your mind about this.

8. What do you think is happening to the DJ at the end? Say why you think this.

9. What time of day is it in this text? Explain how you worked this out.

10. How do you think the author wants you to feel as you read this story? Explain why you think this.

Climbing in the Dark

Imagining

As you read, build up a picture in your head of the setting where this scene takes place. Imagine it in as much detail as you can.

Will is a chimney-sweep who is being mistreated. Tess has come to see if she can rescue him.

Tess Ssh! Will, it's me. Tess.

Will (*Appearing at the bars*)
Ooh, miss. What are you doing 'ere?

Tess I've come to help you. Fry's asleep. You could come out with me now.

Will No, miss. 'E'd beat me rotten…

Tess He won't catch you, Will. If we're quick we can get away and he'll never know.

Will But I can't, miss. The door's locked and 'e's got the keys.

Tess Of course. I saw them on the arm of his chair. If I could just get hold of them…

Will No, 'e'll wake up and there'll be bad trouble for you and all.

Tess But I've got to try something. Wait there.

Will I ain't got no choice, miss. I got to wait 'ere.

Tess Yes, of course.

She creeps over to Fry's chair and very carefully tries to pick up the keys. She gets hold of them but Fry moves in his sleep and puts his hand over them. Gently, gently she pulls them out of his fingers and goes back to Will.

Will   Well done, miss. I thought 'e was waking up just then.

Tess   He will wake up soon. We've got to be quick.

*She unlocks the door and **Will** crawls out. They move slowly past Fry. At the last moment **Fry** stretches and puts his legs out and **Tess** falls over them.*

Fry   (*Waking up*) What? What's going on?

Will   Run, miss! Run!

Fry jumps up and makes a grab at Tess. She squirms out of the way.

Fry   Thief! I'm being robbed!

Tess   Help! Help!

Will   This way! Over here!

*Fry turns and sees Will behind him. He moves slowly towards Will with his arms outstretched. **Will** backs away.*

Fry   Why, it's you, you ratbag!

Tess   Get out, Will! Get out!

Will   I can't leave you here with 'im. 'E's a monster.

Fry   Oh, I'm a monster, am I? Well, I'll show you what monsters do to skinny rats who try to sneak off.

Tess   Leave him alone!

Fry   And you keep quiet, you little thief. I'll deal with you later.

He lunges at Will. **Will** *ducks and runs behind him.* **Fry** *turns round and lunges again. Again he misses and tumbles through the barred door.* **Tess** *shuts the door and locks it.*

Will   Oh, well done, miss! You've locked 'im in 'is own cellar!

Fry   Let me out of here! I'll have your bones for broth, the pair of you!

Tess   Then I certainly shan't let you out, you disgusting man. Come on, Will!

Will *and* **Tess** *run, leaving* **Fry** *to shake the bars and shout.*

Fry   Let me out of here! Let me out!

Climbing in the Dark

Partner activities

I can ...

- read and act out a playscript with my partner
- explain how my character is feeling and why at a given point in the play

1. With your partner, decide who will be Tess and who will be Will. Read the play in your roles and act it out, as far as the point where Fry wakes up.

2. Then explain to your partner how your character is feeling at this point. Draw on clues from the text to help you explain why they feel like this.

Questioning & clarifying

Think about what we know about the characters and the situation from the text, and use your imagination to fill in any gaps.

Think and write

1. Where is Will at the start of the text?

2. Why do you think the first thing Tess says to Will is 'Ssh!'?

3. Why doesn't Will want to escape with Tess at first?

4. Tess calls Will by his first name. Why do you think Will doesn't call Tess by her first name?

5. What happens to wake Fry up?

6. What does Fry think Tess is trying to do?

7. Why doesn't Will want to obey Tess when she says, 'Get out!'?

8. How do the children escape from Fry in the end?

9. What sort of person is Tess? Explain why you think this.

10. Find two speeches in the playscript that you think are particularly effective, and explain why.

Questioning & clarifying

As you are reading, keep asking yourself how Greek religion was different from religions today. How was it similar?

THE GREEK GODS

The Greeks did not believe in just one god. They believed in many gods and goddesses all representing a different aspect of life. These gods were believed to live on Olympus, the highest mountain in Greece, but in the stories that were told they often interfered in the daily lives of their worshippers.

The Greeks believed that the gods were not always kind and good and often caused problems. This helped the Greeks explain why things went wrong in the world around them. The stories they made up about the gods and goddesses were a little like modern soap operas.

The Greeks worshipped their gods and heroes by making sacrifices to them. The worshippers would gather together to kill an animal and burn the fat and bones on a special stone table called an altar. They believed that the gods enjoyed the smell of the burning fat and bones while the Greeks ate the cooked meat themselves. The special days when the sacrifices were held were days off for everyone. This made religion very popular and everyone joined in.

As well as the gods, the Greeks also believed that some men were half man and half god, called heroes. They had superhuman strength and were almost as powerful as the gods. The most well known is Hercules.

Aphrodite – Goddess of love

Apollo – God of the Sun and music

Ares – God of war

Athena – Goddess of wisdom and war

Demeter – Goddess of harvest

Hades – God of the Underworld

Dionysus – God of wine

Zeus – Head of the Gods

Hera – Goddess of marriage and Zeus' wife

Poseidon – God of the Sea

The Greek Gods

Partner activities

I can ...

- find the main points in a piece of text
- with my partner, write a short summary of the text

1. Read the text all through twice. As you read for the second time, make a note of the main point in each paragraph.

2. Using your notes, tell your partner what the main points were. Does your partner agree? Discuss it together.

3. Work together to write a summary of the main points of the whole text, in just two or three sentences.

Summarising

When you are looking for the main points in a paragraph, read the first sentence of the paragraph carefully. It will often help you sum up what the paragraph is about.

Think and write

1. Why do you think the Greeks had more than one god?

2. Where did the Greeks believe their gods lived?

3. Why do you think the author compares the stories about Greek gods with soap operas? Is this an effective comparison? Explain why, or why not.

4. Name two gods and/or goddesses of war.

5. Which two things was Apollo the god of?

6. Why do you think the Greeks were keen on worshipping their gods?

7. When the Greeks sacrificed an animal, which parts were for the gods and which parts did people keep for themselves?

8. What was a Greek hero, and how was he different from ordinary people?

9. Look at the picture on page 17. Why do you think the author included it, and what does it add to the text?

10. Write a caption for the picture on page 16, explaining what it shows.

NEVER WASH YOUR HAIR

Imagining

What do you think Tom (the narrator) has in his hair? Build up a mental picture of them as you read the text.

Headlice live in clean hair. Everyone tells you that. If you don't want headlice, don't wash your hair.

Parents don't understand that. They make you wash your hair, then they complain because you get nits. And I didn't even have any!

I had something else, though.

'There's no shame in having nits,' said Mum, 'so long as you do something about them.'

She was certainly doing something about them. She had me under arrest in the bathroom, with a towel round my neck.

There was steam rising from the hot water in the wash-basin, and the mirror was misting over. She pulled on a pair of white plastic gloves, like a doctor.

'I'm twelve,' I said. 'I don't need you to wash my hair.'

'You do today,' she said.

Next thing I knew my head was in the water and so was most of the towel, and she was rubbing this vile-smelling shampoo – it's called Nit-Death or something – into my head.

When I sat up, I found a dry bit of towel to rub my face with, then I dried the mirror to see what she was doing.

She was bent over my head, searching through my hair.

She had a fixed expression on her face, like a cat at a bird box.

It wasn't so much the look that scared me, it was the nit comb in her hand. I've got curly brown hair, and it hurts when it gets combed.

Especially when Mum does it.

'Ow!' I yelled. It wasn't hurting yet, but I wanted to remind her that I was in there.

'I'm sure these are nits,' said Mum. She raked away with the comb.

'Ouch!' Then I stopped and said nothing. I just sat with my mouth open, looking at the water in the wash-basin.

Something was swimming in there. It wasn't a headlouse. It wasn't much bigger than an ant, but it was definitely

swimming, the way a human swims, with arms and legs.

It had a tawny brown body, and its arms seemed too long for it. It had a long tail, too.

'At least I think these are nits,' said Mum. She didn't sound so sure. 'Is there a magnifying glass in your bedroom?'

'There's my bug viewer,' I said. 'There's a magnifying lens in there.' My eyes were still on the creature. It was nearly at the side of the basin, and it was slowing down.

Mum went away to find the bug viewer.

The creature put out one arm, then the other, and tried to climb up the side of the wash-basin, but there was nothing for it to grip. It scrabbled about and fell back, so I saw its face, and a white patch on its front. It was too exhausted to go on swimming.

I put my finger in the water, just as Mum came in with the lens.

She peered into my hair.

'Funny,' she muttered. 'These are the wrong shape for nits. Wrong colour, too. Curvy and greeny-yellow. Like bananas, only smaller.'

'Can I have the lens, please, Mum?' I said.

The creature had crawled on to my finger, and was shaking itself dry. Then it stopped, and I could feel my heart beating harder and faster. It was rubbing its face with its paws, or hands. I could see its long arms, its sad, ugly, funny face, and its tail.

'There's something moving in there!' said Mum.

She dived at my head, scooped up something with the comb, and dropped it into the bug viewer. 'Give me the lens, Tom, quickly!'

She jammed on the lid, but I was still looking at the creature on my finger. It was crouched down, turning its head one way and then the other. Mum noticed it, too.

'That's another one,' she said. 'It must be some kind of headlouse. Where on earth have you been, to pick these up?'

'Just school,' I said. 'And Nick and I went looking for red squirrels last weekend. Are you going to ring his mum?'

'I'll have to,' she said, 'in case Nick's caught them, too. Don't worry, I'm sure she won't tell anyone. But if you've got nits, she needs to know.'

'No, Mum,' I said.

'Sorry, but she has to be told.'

'I meant, no, I haven't got nits. I've got head monkeys. Look!'

Never Wash Your Hair

Partner activities

I can ...

- discuss what will happen next in a text
- write a story plan for the next part of the text

1. Read the text, and think about what you would do next if you were Tom (the narrator) or his mum. Is Tom right about the things in his hair? What will happen? Discuss it with your partner.

2. Agree with your partner on a series of events that might happen next. Together, write a story plan to show how the story might develop.

Predicting

Think about the characters and what they are like – how would you react if you were Tom? Would Tom and his mum react the same way? What might the problems be?

Think and write

1. Why does Tom's mum feel she has to wash his hair?

2. Why does Tom say his mum 'had me under arrest in the bathroom'?

3. Tom says his mum 'had a fixed expression on her face, like a cat at a bird box'. Is this an effective comparison? Explain why, or why not.

4. Why is Tom scared when he sees the nit comb?

5. Why does Tom think the thing in the wash-basin isn't a nit or a headlouse?

6. What do Tom and his mum use to have a closer look at the things in Tom's hair?

7. Why does Tom's mum decide to ring Nick's mum?

8. Find two clues that help explain why Tom thinks he has head monkeys.

9. What might Tom's mum say when she sees the head monkeys? Write the conversation between Tom and mum.

10. Look at the first three paragraphs. Do they make an effective opening? Explain why, or why not.

AIR RAID!

Summarising

When you have read the text, think of one sentence to sum up what happens.

Old Tin Hat, the air raid warden, was on duty. It was his job to keep people out of the way until the bomb disposal team arrived. He had roped off the site, and no one could get anywhere near the bomb.

He always chased the boys off. 'You'll get killed, one day!' he'd yell.

But the boys took no notice. Exploring bomb sites was an exciting game, and escaping from Old Tin Hat made it even better.

'Do you think he's scared?' asked Jack.

'No, not Old Tin Hat. He's got no feelings,' said Harry. 'Keep your head down, Jack, we don't want him to see us. You know what he's like – he'll start yelling.'

Old Tin Hat moved away to check some ropes, and the boys pulled themselves to the edge. They had another look at the bomb.

'Why doesn't the bomb disposal come?' asked Jack.

'Too busy,' said Harry. 'They won't defuse this until the morning. Not much to blow up here anyway – most of it's already gone.'

Harry was right. As the brothers gazed round them, they saw heaps of rubble and big holes everywhere. Bits of walls were standing, many of them scorched black by fire. Here and there, scraps of once lovely curtains hung limp and sad.

Harry pointed towards the river. Some seagulls were having a party on an ancient piano which had landed down near the water. A chair was perched crazily on someone's chimney. Earth and brick dust covered everything.

Suddenly Jack felt cold.

'Aw! Come on, Harry. Let's go.'

Air Raid!

Partner activities

I can ...

- find clues to help work out what characters think
- use these clues in a role-play

1. Read the text, and then talk with your partner about how Jack and Harry feel about the bomb site. Find clues in the text to help you work this out.

2. Choose a character – either Jack or Harry. Your partner should ask you questions to find out how your character feels about the excitement and danger of the bomb site. Be honest about your character's real feelings.

Imagining

Try to think yourself into the head of your character, using clues about him from the text. What would he want to do?

Think and write

1. Where are Jack and Harry, at the start of the text?

2. What are they doing there?

3. Why has the air raid warden roped the area off?

4. What is the air raid warden's nickname, and how do you think he got it?

5. What do the boys do when the air raid warden shouts at them? Is this sensible, or not? Explain why.

6. Write a paragraph to describe the bomb site, or draw a labelled picture of it.

7. Pick one descriptive phrase from the text that you think is effective, and explain why.

8. What two reasons does Harry suggest to explain why the bomb disposal team hasn't come yet?

9. Why (apart from the weather) do you think Jack suddenly feels cold at the end?

10. Imagine the air raid warden catches the boys. Write a conversation between them.

ANTARCTIC ADVENTURE

Imagining

As you read, think about what the text is telling you about the Antarctic landscape. Try to build up a clear picture of it in your mind.

Ranulph Fiennes and Mike Stroud watched the ski-plane buzz away from them. When it disappeared from view they slowly fixed the sledge harnesses to their waists and shoulders and stared out at the nothingness all around them. This was the moment of truth. Were the sledges too heavy to pull? Would they move at all? Until now they hadn't tried them. It would be like pulling four of your mates in a bathtub from Edinburgh to London and back in the freezing cold.

The straps creaked. Bit by bit they inched forward. It was possible – just.

At last they were on their way. To begin with, the weather was good; the only problem was a broken flask. The worst thing was pulling those heavy sledges day after day. Sometimes the thought of pulling them a few more metres was bad enough. The fact they had to haul them across the Antarctic began to make them angry and depressed.

After a while, Ranulph came to think of his sledge as a horrible monster that needed slaying. That thought kept him going every time his skis slid backwards on the ice.

Almost immediately, the harness straps began digging into their hips like sharp knives and the stiff waistbands rubbed their skin raw.

Soon, Ranulph twisted his shoulder blades. But the pain was easy compared to the boredom. That really drove them crazy. Have you ever spent a day staring at nothing but your bedroom carpet? Imagine then, weeks staring at nothing except snow and ice.

They agreed to share the navigation. It's very hard *always* following! When you lead, you're busy working out the best route across the ice using the compass. You're scanning the land, sizing up problems the whole time. You've got something to do. Something to think about. When you're following there's nothing to do. Nothing to think about. And it drives you mad.

They swapped over the lead position every so often. Ranulph (who was always used to being the leader) got more and more annoyed every time it was Mike's turn to be in front. Mike was fitter, smaller, and eleven years younger, so he always covered more distance when he was out in front.

This led to problems. Ranulph said Mike was going too fast. He was wasting energy and using too many calories. They only had so much food to last the journey. They couldn't afford to lose too much weight. But Mike enjoyed pushing himself. He hated plodding along behind, especially when Ranulph changed track and Mike couldn't see a reason for it.

Facts about Antarctica

Forty million (40,000,000) years ago Antarctica was covered in trees.

Twenty million (20,000,000) years ago there was extensive ice.

Twelve million (12,000,000) years ago the great ice sheet had started to form.

The poles are so cold due to the low angle of the sun which means they get about 40% less sun than the equator.

Antarctic Adventure

Partner activities

I can ...

- identify non-fiction features in a text
- discuss how this text is similar to and different from a fiction text

1. As you read the text, make notes on the main non-fiction features you spot. Discuss this with your partner and together draw up a list of all the non-fiction features.

2. In what ways is this text a bit like a fiction text? With your partner, make a chart to show ways in which the text is like a non-fiction text, and ways in which it is like a fiction text.

Predicting

Think about what you would expect to find in a non-fiction text. How does this text match up to your expectations?

Think and write

1. At the start of this text, what stage in their expedition are Ranulph and Mike at? How do you know?

2. What do you think was on the sledges?

3. Why does the author say that when Ranulph and Mike put on the sledge harnesses for the first time, 'This was the moment of truth'?

4. What does the author compare to the task of pulling the sledges? Is this a good comparison? Explain why, or why not.

5. Why do you think Ranulph thought of his sledge as a horrible monster? How might this have helped him?

6. Name three problems that Ranulph and Mike had on their expedition.

7. Which do you think was the biggest problem, and why?

8. Why did Ranulph get annoyed when it was Mike's turn to lead? Explain why.

9. Why did Mike like being in the lead?

10. Think of an effective new title for the text.

The Moonlit Stream

A stream far off beneath the moon
    Flowed silver-bright and thin,
Winding its way like some slow tune
    Played on a violin.

The valley trees were hushed and still;
    The sky was pearly grey;
The moonlight slept upon the hill –
    As white as snow it lay.

Then softly from a ruined tower
    That rose beside the stream
A bell chimed out the midnight hour;
    And then – Oh, did I dream? –

Then all at once a long, black boat
    With neither sail nor oars
Down that bright stream began to float
    Between its shadowy shores.

Imagining

As you read, build up a picture in your head of the scene that the poet describes. Don't forget to imagine the sounds he describes as well. What is the atmosphere of the poem like?

No passenger nor steersman stirred
    On that enchanting thing;
But faint, unearthly-sweet, I heard
    A choir of voices sing.

It moved mysterious and serene,
    A sable-feathered swan;
It seemed the soul of some sad queen
    Was borne to Avalon.

So in my thoughts that shadowy boat
    Will sail the moonlit river,
And faintly, I shall hear the note
    Of that sad choir for ever.

James Reeves

The Moonlit Stream

Partner activities

I can ...

- describe the mood and atmosphere of a poem
- find some quotations that help to convey the mood and atmosphere

1. Read the poem, and then think about how it makes you feel. Share your ideas with your partner.

2. Together, list words and phrases that describe the mood and atmosphere of the poem. Find two or three quotations from the poem that show the mood and atmosphere.

3. Choose your favourite quotation and explain why you think it conveys the mood and atmosphere.

Summarising

Read the poem, and then close the book and think about how you felt as you read it. Did your feelings change as you read?

Think and write

1. What does the poet compare the stream to, in the first verse?

2. Do you think this is an effective comparison? Why, or why not?

3. Apart from the poet, are there any other people or other living things in the poem? Explain your answer.

4. What sound comes from the ruined tower?

5. What does the poet compare the long, black boat to? Is it a good comparison?

6. What is strange about the long, black boat?

7. What does the poet suggest might be on the boat?

8. Look at the first verse. Which lines rhyme? Do the other verses follow the same rhyming pattern?

9. Think of three words to describe the atmosphere of this poem, and explain why you chose them.

10. Why do you think the author chose the title 'The Moonlit Stream'? Think of another effective title.

The Worst Team in the World

Predicting

Before you read, have
a quick look at the text
and artwork and predict
what kind of story you
think it will be.

Reject Rovers were losing. Nothing new in that, but
now they were on the attack. It always made
their forwards nervous, especially
Kevin 'Panic' Taylor.

By pure luck the ball had landed at his feet and
he was wondering what to do with it. Kevin was
just outside the penalty area and had a clear
run on goal.

Coxley Colts' goalkeeper got hopefully to his
feet. He'd been sitting down, bored to death for
the last fifty minutes, without a single shot to save. He came off
his line and crouched ready to fling himself at Kevin's shot – if it
ever came.

'Steady. No need to panic. Keep calm,' Kevin told himself.

He could see the back of the net and imagined the way it would
quiver when the ball went in. If only he could just keep cool and for
once – just for once – score a goal for Rovers.

'Shoot, Kevin! Shoot!' shouted Mr Turnbull from the touchline.

'Pass, Kevin!' yelled Persil. Kevin looked up. He would have liked to
pass. Someone else could gladly have the job of shooting. But as usual
Persil was hovering way out by the corner flag. He never came near
the penalty area in case he got his kit dirty. It was all down to Kevin.

He could hear Colts' defenders pounding back to tackle him. Any
second now a leg would lunge out and scoop the ball away to safety.

The chance would be gone. It was now or never. Kevin glanced up at the goal to take aim. And that was when the familiar panic set in. The goal seemed to shrink to Subbuteo size and the crouching goalkeeper grew hands like shovels.

Kevin felt hot and dizzy. He was sweating. When he swung his right leg back it felt like it was set in concrete. His toe connected with something hard … it was the ground and Kevin fell flat on his face. The ball trundled harmlessly into the goalkeeper's gloves. (Kevin saw the disappointment on his face.) …

The Colts' goalkeeper kicked the ball upfield. It bounced once on the halfway line. Stringbean, Rejects' central defender, jumped to head it, but too early. His lanky body – all knees and elbows – went down as the ball was going up. It bounced over his head and one of Colts' strikers ran on to collect it.

There was only Rejects' goalkeeper, Scuba, to beat. He stayed on his line. Scuba never came out in case someone dribbled round him and made him look stupid. He preferred to look stupid in his goal. But he always dived with great style – that's why the team called him Scuba.

The Colts' striker shot and the ball soared towards the right hand top corner. Scuba dived spectacularly towards the bottom left hand corner. The ball bulged in the net. The Colts' striker grinned and shook his head in disbelief. He shook hands with his team mates. There wasn't too much celebration. After all, it was his fifth goal that afternoon and the score was 11-0. The referee blew his whistle soon after.

'Bad luck, lad,' he said to Kevin, picking up the match ball. 'Someone's got to lose. You lot make it look easy.'

'Yeah,' said Kevin, 'we've had a lot of practice.'

The Worst Team in the World

Partner activities

I can ...

- work out how the main character's emotions change during the text
- draw a 'feelings graph' to show this

1. Read the text, and talk with your partner about how Kevin's feelings change as the story goes on. Write notes about how he feels at each stage.

2. Working with your partner, draw a 'feelings graph' to show how Kevin's feelings go up and down in the text. Alternatively, one of you can take the role of Kevin and the other person can ask him what were the best and worst moments for him.

Questioning & clarifying

Keep asking yourself how Kevin feels at each stage in the story. Sometimes the text tells you, and sometimes you have to work it out yourself.

Think and write

1. How is Kevin feeling at the start of the text, and why?

2. Why do you think Kevin's team is called Reject Rovers?

3. Find three quotes from the text that show how good (or not!) Reject Rovers are.

4. 'Coxley Colts' goalkeeper got hopefully to his feet'. Why do you think he was feeling hopeful?

5. Why couldn't Kevin pass to Persil?

6. Find a sentence in the text where the author describes how things look to Kevin when he is panicking. Is this an effective description? Explain why, or why not.

7. Who do you think Mr Turnbull is?

8. Kevin and his team-mates all have nicknames. Pick two of the nicknames and explain why they are appropriate.

9. What happens when the Colts' striker takes a shot at the Rejects' goal?

10. Are the Colts excited at the end of the match? Explain why, or why not.

Questioning & clarifying

As you read, ask yourself – what advantages do robots have over humans, when it comes to doing difficult and dangerous work?

Robots: Difficult and Dangerous Work

Robots are especially useful in difficult and dangerous situations.

They can be built to:
- cope with radioactivity
- be very strong
- cope with very hot or very cold places.

And they:
- don't breathe air, so can be exposed to smoke and poisonous gas
- might break, but they can't die.

Difficult situations
Robots help scientists to explore the frozen Arctic, Antarctica and the depths of the oceans.

Dangerous situations
Robots help to clear mine fields.

34

The operator stands behind thick lead glass and lets the robot arms pack this radioactive material.

The worst radioactive disaster of all time was when, in 1986, a nuclear reactor at the power station at Chernobyl, Ukraine, exploded. Twenty years later the station is still highly radioactive. More than 100,000 people had to leave their homes and many have not been able to go back home yet. Land as far away as Wales, UK, was contaminated with radioactivity.

For many years people were sent into the remains of the station to test the levels of radioactivity, but the levels were still so high that this was very dangerous, even in special suits. Since 1999, robot *Pioneer* has been making trips into the remains instead. Robots may help to clear up the station in the future.

Robots: Difficult and Dangerous Work

Partner activities

I can ...

- sum up the main message of the text
- work with my partner to make the shortest possible summary of the text

1. Read the text and take notes on the main point in each paragraph or section.
2. Sum up the main point of the whole text for your partner, in just two or three sentences.
3. Challenge your partner to come up with a shorter summary. Take it in turns to see how short a summary you can make.

Summarising

Focus on the most important aspects of the text – you can leave out anything that is just a detail. Remember that your summary still has to make sense, though!

Think and write

1. Find three reasons why robots might be better than people for doing difficult and dangerous work.
2. Find one way in which robots can help scientists.
3. Why might it be better to use a robot than a human to help clear a mine field?
4. What happened at Chernobyl in 1986?
5. What job do robots do at Chernobyl?
6. What are the dangers for people at Chernobyl?
7. Why do you think the author chose to include information about Chernobyl in this text?
8. What do you think the large photo on page 34 shows?
9. Why did the author choose to include the large photo on page 35?
10. Do you think that robots would always be better than people at working in difficult and dangerous situations? Explain why you think this.

From *Trapped!* by Malachy Doyle,
TreeTops Fiction Stage 14 More Stories A, pages 55–63

Trapped!

Tom's dog Jacko is trapped in an old mineshaft. Tom abseils down with the rescue team.

Jacko spotted me above him and started barking like mad.

'Shush, Jacko.'

Before I'd got myself free of the straps, he was jumping all over me, licking my face, my hands. And I was just as pleased to see him.

'Right, Jacko,' I explained calmly. 'We've got to get you out of here. We're going to put you in this sling and lift you up.' But he pulled away and ran off down the passage. Helen shone her torch after him. He was standing still, watching me.

'Come here, Jacko!' I said in my sternest voice. He crawled towards me.

'OK, everyone,' I told the others. 'Let's get him in.'

But quick as a flash he broke away once more, into the darkness.

I was just about to yell at him again when it clicked what was happening. He wanted me to follow him. Of course!

'What is it, Jacko? Is there something down there?'

I went after him. Somewhere behind me I could hear the others. Dave was telling Ali what was going on over the radio.

In the torch light, with Dad beside me, I followed Jacko along the passage. It sloped steeply down. The air was getting colder all the time.

Jacko disappeared through a narrow hole in the rock. We waited for Dave to go through first, just in case.

On the other side, we found ourselves in a great underground room, with a vast lake in the middle. Jacko waited till everyone was through. Then he led us around the edge of the lake to a large rock and went behind it. We followed him and there, in a shaft of light from another hole high above, lay a man.

I pulled back, frightened, but Dad rushed over to him. 'It's Will Evans!' he gasped. 'Are you all right, Will?' There was no answer.

Helen reached him and knelt by the twisted body, feeling Will's pulse, checking for a heartbeat. Then she ripped off her coat and wrapped it around the old man.

'He's alive all right, but only just,' she said. 'Hypothermia by the look of it, never mind any injuries from the fall.'

Our eyes turned upwards to the daylight, way above us, at the top of the narrow shaft. 'We've got to get him out of here, quick.'

'What's hypothermia?' I asked Dad.

'It means his body's much too cold. They'll have to get him to hospital as soon as possible.' Dave was already on the radio to Ali, asking her to call in the helicopter.

'Well I know who the real star of the show is,' said Ali, when all the excitement was over. We were sitting round the table with steaming hot bowls of Mam's best stew in front of us.

'Who's that then?' Dad asked.

'Tom's dog,' she answered. 'If he hadn't heard poor old Will calling and gone to the rescue, that man'd be dead. No doubt about it.'

'So he's Tom's dog now, is he?' said Dad with a smile, ruffling my hair. And for the very first time I got the feeling that he really knew Jacko belonged to me.

Trapped!

Partner activities

I can ...

- understand the emotions of characters in a story
- use a role-play to help explore these emotions

1. Read the text. Then, with your partner, take the roles of Tom and Dad, and act out the story up to the point where they find Will Evans.

2. Freeze the action at that point, and take turns to explain what is going through your character's head. What does each of you think will happen next? What do you each think you should do, and why?

Questioning & clarifying

As you read, keep thinking about how your character would be feeling and why. Use what you know about them from the text, and also your own imagination.

Think and write

1. Where is Tom at the start, and what is he doing?

2. Why doesn't Jacko want to get in the sling and go back up with Tom?

3. What are the names of the three people who help Tom and Dad to rescue Jacko?

4. Why do you think Tom waits for Dave to go first through the hole in the rock? Is this a sensible thing to do?

5. How does Tom feel when they first see Will Evans, and why might he feel like this?

6. Why does Dave ask Ali to call the helicopter?

7. Who does Ali say is 'the real star of the show'? Do you think she is right? Explain why, or why not.

8. What is the relationship between Tom and Jacko like? Quote evidence from the text to show this.

9. Find a quotation from the text that helps to create a feeling of suspense.

10. What do you think Dad thinks about Jacko being called 'Tom's dog'?

Questioning & clarifying

As you read, think about who the poet is, and try to work out what he is trying to tell us in this poem. It may help if you read the poem out loud, slowly.

Alabama

My brethren,
among the legends of my people
it is told how a chief,
leading the remnant of his people,
crossed a great river,
and striking his tipi-stake upon
the ground,
exclaimed, "A-la-ba-ma!"
This in our language means
"Here we may rest!"
But he saw not the future.
The white man came:
he and his people could not rest there;
they were driven out,
and in a dark swamp
they were thrust down into the slime
and killed.
The word he so sadly spoke
has given a name to one of the white
man's states.
There is no spot under those stars
that now smile upon us,
where the Indian can plant his foot
and sigh "A-la-ba-ma."

Khe-Tha-A-Hi (Eagle Wing)

Alabama

I can ...

- work out the message of a poem
- write a speech to present the message to a different audience

1. Read the poem silently, and then again out loud.

2. Together, make notes about what the poet, Khe-Tha-A-Hi, is saying. What does he tell us about the history of Alabama, and how does he feel about what happened?

3. Use your notes to write a speech explaining to the 'white man' what happened and why it was important. Suggest what could be done to help put things right.

Summarising

When you are working out the message of the poem, think about what actually happened, and about how people felt about it.

Think and write

1. Who is this poem addressed to?

2. What does 'A-la-ba-ma' mean in the poet's language?

3. What other meaning does the word 'Alabama' have?

4. Which words show us that the chief did not have all of his people with him when he crossed the river?

5. Was the chief right when he first said 'A-la-ba-ma'? Explain your answer.

6. What happened when the white man came?

7. Why do you think the poet called this poem 'Alabama'? Do you think this makes a good title for the poem? Explain why, or why not.

8. What does the poet feel life is like now for him and his people? Quote some words that help to show this.

9. How does this poem make you feel? Explain why.

10. Why do you think the poet chose to write this text as a poem, rather than as a letter or a persuasive speech?

Tomahawk Beckwourth

Questioning & clarifying

What sort of person is Tomahawk Beckwourth? Look out for clues as you read the text.

First off, I'll describe myself, so you've got some sort of picture of me to carry in your head. I'm what many folk describe as a hardscrabble sort of man.

I dress in fringed buckskin shirts, leggings and moccasins and I stand two metres tall. My black hair is long and at one time it reached past my waist. My skin's black too, but not as black as my hair, and over the years it's been scarred by bullets, arrows and war-axes.

My ears are pierced and I wear gold earrings and chains and braid my hair or tie it with ribbons. I'm strong and muscular and I'm a cheerful sort of man who enjoys singing and having a laugh.

As to my skills, they're many: I speak English, French and Spanish – and Indian languages too. I know the Indian ways better than anyone and can track, hunt and scout. I'm expert with dagger, tomahawk and gun and a skilful horseman who knows all manner of tricks. I can ride a galloping horse bareback, then hang upside down so my hair brushes the earth.

Now I'll tell you a bit about my folks. My daddy was Sir Jennings Beckwourth whose family came from England to America, generations back. He was an educated man with noble ancestors going back to the days of the Norman Conquest. My great grand-daddy (times about fifty, I reckon!) helped William whip Harold at the Battle of Hastings in 1066 and was rewarded with a title and lands. Which is why my own Pa was a Sir … God rest his soul.

My Ma wasn't nearly so high falutin' as my Pa. She was a black slave whose family had been brought to America from Africa to work on the plantations. I don't exactly know how they met, but they got together and had little me.

Tomahawk Beckwourth

I can ...

- make notes about a character in a text
- use my notes to create a detailed character profile

1. Read the text, and then talk with your partner about Tomahawk Beckwourth – what sort of person was he? What did he look like, and what did he do? Reread the text carefully and make notes on this.

2. Together, create a detailed character profile for Tomahawk Beckwourth. Use clues, and quotations from the text. Add a picture of him in action! Finish with a short paragraph to sum up his character.

Summarising

Try to think of the two or three most important things about Tomahawk Beckwourth – the things that make him most memorable.

Think and write

1. When do you think Tomahawk Beckwourth lived – now or in the past? What makes you think this?

2. Think of three words to describe him and explain why you chose them.

3. Why do you think Tomahawk Beckwourth calls himself 'a hardscrabble sort of man'? Is this a good description? Why?

4. What kinds of clothes does he wear?

5. Find two unusual things about Tomahawk Beckwourth's appearance.

6. What does he know about the Indian ways?

7. How do you think Tomahawk Beckwourth got his name?

8. What does he mean by: 'My Ma wasn't nearly so high falutin' as my Pa'?

9. What was his father's name, and how did his father get his title?

10. What style of writing does the author use, and why do you think he chose it? What effect does it have on you as a reader?

The Powder Monkey

Predicting

What type of story do you think this is, judging from the first couple of paragraphs?

Harry and Billy have been at sea with Lord Nelson's fleet, and took part in the Battle of Trafalgar. Now they are returning home.

Harry dragged Billy forward to meet his ma.

She was charmed immediately by his cheeky grin.

'You must stay with us,' Harry heard her say.

Shadrach and Mr Mumford came over and shook Harry by the hand. Shadrach slapped him on the shoulder. 'Well, I suppose earning tuppence a day will be too tame for you now, eh?' he said.

'No, sir. I'll start again tomorrow if I can bring Billy too,' Harry said. The men laughed.

'You mean you're not signing up for another sea trip?' Mr Mumford said.

Harry blushed, but said nothing.

'Well, before you go off home,' the gunsmith went on, 'I've got something for you back at the shop.'

In the back room, Mr Mumford took the sampler down from the wall. He pointed to the beautifully embroidered words.

'There's no place like home,' he said. 'Let this remind you.'

He handed it to Harry. Harry thanked him.

He knew he didn't really need it. He had his own reminders; too many of them. His dreams would be filled with them.

They'd be very different to the dreams he'd had before going to sea and to war. And he never wanted to handle a gun again, unless it was to clean it.

The Powder Monkey

I can ...

- read a text and summarise the main things that happen
- create a cartoon strip or storyboard to show what happens in the story

1. Read the text, and then shut the book and take turns with your partner to try to sum up the main points of the story. Make notes of two or three main things that happen.

2. Use your notes to help you make a cartoon strip or storyboard that tells the story, with just two or three pictures. Use speech bubbles and captions too.

Summarising

Think about which parts of the story are most important, and which just add detail. You can leave out anything that just adds detail.

Think and write

1. When do you think this story is set? Find some evidence in the text.

2. Where do you think Billy and Harry are at the start of the text?

3. How do you think Harry and Billy feel at the start of the text?

4. What kind of person is Harry? Explain why you think this.

5. What job does Mr Mumford do?

6. What does Harry's ma think of Billy?

7. Who do you think Shadrach is, judging from evidence in the text?

8. What does Mr Mumford give Harry, and why?

9. Why do you think Harry 'never wanted to handle a gun again'?

10. Whose point of view is this story told from, and how do you know?

Predicting

How many different ways of presenting information can you find on this page? What type of text do you think it is?

TRIREMES

The Greeks' best fighting ship was the trireme, so called because it had three tiers of oars. It was powered by 170 rowers, sitting on benches on the ship's three decks. Designed to be fast and lethal, it was built to ram and sink enemy ships. The trireme was also a mobile platform for the spearmen and archers who lined its decks, ready to pelt the enemy with spears and arrows.

TRIREME

KEY DATA

LENGTH 40 metres

HEIGHT 3 metres

WIDTH 6 metres

TOP SPEED 14 knots

CREW 14 spearmen, 4 archers, 25 officers, 170 rowers

KEY BATTLE VICTORY
Salamis, 480BC against Persia

KEY STRENGTHS
speed, manoeuvrability.

BATTLE TACTIC
diekplous (break through and ram)

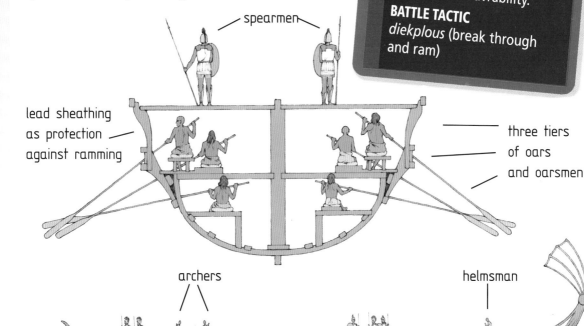

spearmen

lead sheathing as protection against ramming

three tiers of oars and oarsmen

archers

helmsman

bronze sheeting for strength when ramming

pine, fir or cedar bodywork

47

Triremes

Partner activities

I can ...

- understand information presented in different forms
- use this information to draw a detailed picture

1. Read the text, and then discuss how triremes were used and what advantages they gave to the Greeks. What disadvantages might there have been? What would it be like to row one?

2. With your partner, draw a detailed picture of a trireme in action in a battle. Include as much information from the text as you can. Write a caption for your picture.

Imagining

When you draw your picture, think about what it would have been like to be part of the crew of a trireme. What would you do, see, hear and feel?

Think and write

1. Why do you think the trireme has 'tri' as part of its name?

2. What powered triremes so that they could move through the water?

3. How did triremes help Greeks in the battle against enemy ships and soldiers? Find two ways.

4. What kinds of weapons were used by Greek soldiers on triremes?

5. Where was bronze sheeting used on a trireme, and why?

6. What was the main body of a trireme made of?

7. How many decks did a trireme have?

8. How many people in total would travel on a trireme?

9. Look at the 'key data' box. Why do you think the author chose to present it like this?

10. Why do you think the author decided to include a cut-away diagram in the text? What do you think this adds to the text?

One Girl School

Marnover Village Hall was crammed full of people. Up on the stage was Mrs Whiffy, Head of Marnover Village School, and behind her was a banner: MARNOVER SCHOOL MUST NOT CLOSE. In front of her were rows of angry parents, confused kids and screaming babies. Right at the back of the hall, chewing on a stale bit of gum, looking really bored, was me.

My name is Bernie Lee. That's short for Bernadette, except no one calls me Bernadette unless they want a close-up view of my fist. My mum moved to this stupid village after she split up with Dad. We used to live in Grosshampton, which is a nice big city where the air is ninety-nine per cent petrol fumes. Mum decided it was better to live in the country, so my brain wouldn't get full of poison. Having poison in your brain makes you very poorly and also thick. That's my excuse, anyway.

As I was saying, Mrs Whiffy was up on stage making a speech. She obviously wasn't used to talking to grown-ups and now and again told someone off for looking out of the window. But everyone did as they were told because once upon a time Mrs Whiffy had taught them all and they still seemed a bit scared of her.

'Marnover School,' said Mrs Whiffy, 'has served this village for generations. Marnover School is cosy, comfy, cuddly and *traditional*. But the council says it's too small. The council wants to send your children to Bigtown Monster Primary, which is huge, faceless, fowsty and fifteen miles away!' There was a howl of protest from the parents.

'I've heard there are sixty-five pupils in every class!' one cried.

'Yes!' called another. 'And some children have been lost for weeks in the corridors!'

'Exactly,' said Mrs Whiffy. 'Which is why we must save Marnover School!' There was a huge round of applause.

Mrs Whiffy hushed the crowd. 'We need some volunteers to take round a petition,' she said, and explained to the children that a petition was a letter of protest that everybody put their name on.

Mrs Whiffy's eagle eyes scanned the room and, to my horror, fell on me. 'You at the back!' she cried. 'You, chewing the gum!' Of course, Mrs Whiffy knew the names of all her pupils, but I hadn't even started at the school yet. If I had my way I never would.

'I've got a bad arm, Miss,' I said.

'That's all right,' said Mrs Whiffy. 'You only need one arm to carry a petition.'

So that's how I got my first (unpaid) job in Marnover village. Mum said it was an excellent chance to meet all the interesting local people, and if I was lucky they might give me some local cheese or home-made rhubarb-and-ginger jam.

I sulked for a few days, then I had an idea. What if I kind of, you know, put people off signing the petition? Then, with any luck, the school would close and I'd go to that nice, big modern place in Bigtown after all. Well, it was worth a shot.

I started at Old Appletree Cottage which had a thatched roof, roses round the door and a surround-sound, home-cinema telly in the front room. A woman with a posh voice answered the door. That didn't surprise me. No one seemed to speak in oo-arr country accents in Marnover.

'I'd like you to sign a petition to save Marnover School,' I announced.

'Certainly!' she replied.

'Why should we go to Bigtown Monster Primary?' I said.

'Yes, why should you?' chimed the woman.

'Just because it's got the best exam results in the country,' I added.

'I beg your pardon?' said the woman.

We talked a little more and, funnily enough, she changed her mind about signing the petition. My next stop was the vicarage, where Mr Fuggles the vicar invited me in for tea and scones.

'I wasn't too keen on Marnover School at first,' I admitted, 'but when I heard they were going to have a school disco blasting out five hundred watts of bass-booming hip-hop I changed my mind completely.'

'Five hundred watts of *what*?' said the vicar, spraying crumbs all over me. For some reason, he didn't want to sign either. This petition wasn't going well at all. I decided to call next at Old Farm Road. It's funny they call it Old Farm Road because it's full of brand spanking-new houses. You'd think that would mean there'd be tons of kids for the village school. But the houses are all full of retired people which means they're at least ninety.

I called on a nice old couple in a chalet bungalow.

'Sign the petition?' they said. 'Of course we'll sign the petition!'

'Thank goodness for that,' I said. 'The rest of the village has refused to sign.'

The couple looked at the blank page and frowns crossed their faces.

'Makes you wonder if they know something we don't,' I said.

The frowns grew stronger. 'What do you think that could be?' they asked.

I shrugged.

'Maybe we ought to leave it,' they said.

'Suit yourselves,' I replied.

One Girl School

Partner activities

I can ...

- act out a scene based on part of a text
- write out my scene as a playscript

1. With your partner, pretend to be Bernie and one of the people she calls on to sign the petition. Act out the conversation between them. You can use words from the text, but also add some more lines of your own to make the conversation sound convincing.

2. Together, write out your scene as a brief playscript. You could then swap with another pair and act out the scene they have written!

Predicting

Use what you know about Bernie from the text to help you decide what she would say.

Think and write

1. What is Bernie's full name, and what does she think of it?

2. Does Bernie like living in Marnover? Why, or why not?

3. What does Bernie's mum like about Marnover?

4. Look at Mrs Whiffy's speeches at the meeting. Find some quotes using persuasive language.

5. Do you think Mrs Whiffy's speeches were effective in persuading her audience? Quote some evidence from the text to show this.

6. What job does Mrs Whiffy give Bernie at the meeting, and what do you think Bernie thinks of this?

7. What does Bernie decide to do about the petition, and why?

8. Does Bernie's idea work?

9. Why do you think the author decided to make Bernie the narrator of the story?

10. What kind of person is Bernie? Write a paragraph to describe her.

Imagining

This poem describes a scene very clearly. As you read, try to build up a picture of it in your head.

Westward! Westward!

From *The Song of Hiawatha*

On the shore stood Hiawatha,
Turned and waved his hand at parting;
On the clear and luminous water
Launched his birch-canoe for sailing,
From the pebbles of the margin
Shoved it forth into the water;
Whispered to it, 'Westward! westward!'
And with speed it darted forward.

And the evening sun descending
Set the clouds on fire with redness,
Burned the broad sky, like a prairie,
Left upon the level water
One long track and trail of splendour,
Down whose stream, as down a river,
Westward, westward Hiawatha
Sailed into the fiery sunset,
Sailed into the purple vapours,
Sailed into the dusk of evening.

H W Longfellow

Westward! Westward!

Partner activities

I can ...

- read a poem and talk about its mood and what it is about
- use my voice and sound effects to create a dramatic reading

1. Talk about the poem with your partner. What happens? What pictures do you see in your head when you read it? What is the mood of the poem, and how does it make you feel?

2. With your partner, practise reading the poem aloud. You could add movement, sound effects or musical instruments to accompany your reading. Rehearse it several times, and then perform it or tape it.

Questioning & clarifying

If there is anything you don't understand in the poem, try rereading it out loud, or discuss it with your partner.

Think and write

1. What is happening in this poem? Try to sum it up in one sentence.

2. What method of transport does Hiawatha use in the poem?

3. What time is it in the poem? Find a quote to show this.

4. Do you think the title 'Westward! Westward!' is an effective one for this poem? Explain why, or why not.

5. Think of another title that could be used for this poem.

6. The text says that Hiawatha sailed down 'one long track and trail of splendour'. What was this track?

7. Reread the poem and then close the book. Draw a picture of the scene you can see in your head when you think about the poem.

8. How would you describe the mood or atmosphere of the poem?

9. What do you notice about the rhythm of this poem?

10. What kind of effect do you think the rhythm has on you as you read the poem?

MACBETH

Imagining

What would it be like to be in the place described in this text? What would you feel, hear, see …?

I am, I think, fifteen years old. I was born with marks upon me which some called signs of witchcraft. When sickness came to the village I was blamed, tormented, and sentenced to death. I escaped and fled to the wild heath, to live on berries and to spend my life watching.

Most of all I watch those women they call the Weird Sisters because, like me, they are called witches. The sisters have the knowledge I seek. They can conjure up storms, cast curses on their enemies, and greatest of all, foretell the future.

It was from the sisters that I first heard the name Macbeth. What a foul day that was! Thunder rattled the heavens and fog smothered the heath like a shroud. The sisters danced wildly, screaming about a bloody battle and showing off a hacked-off thumb. Again and again they shrieked the name 'Macbeth'.

As the sisters melted into the fog I crept forward to view their glass. Within this sacred object all things on earth could be seen – or, at least, all things the sisters wished to see.

With heart beating hard I steadied my eye. First I saw the fluttering flags of the King of Norway, then the face of Cawdor, the traitor lord, in arms against the Scots king, Duncan. Suddenly, confusion filled the glass, then horror. Screams, curses, and blasting cannons out-roared the thunder. I saw horsemen with axes hacking. I saw limbs chopped from bodies. I watched living people dropping like dumb puppets. Then, in the midst of it all, I spied a superman.

He stood like a rock in a heaving sea, slashing and hacking with

awesome power. Alone, it seemed, he turned the tide. The flags of Norway turned and fled, and the day was Scotland's.

Soon I was to crouch within a few yards of the hero of this battle.

One dark evening, the Weird Sisters gathered at their appointed place. By and by a tired army arrived, creaking and clanking across the rainswept heath. Out of their number rode two men, one our hero. Seeing the sisters, they came to a halt. They had seen many horrors that day, but nothing quite like these wild and bearded women.

'All hail, Macbeth!' cried the first sister. 'Hail to thee, Thane of Glamis!' So this was Macbeth! I felt awe and a sense of foreboding.

'All hail, Macbeth!' cried the second sister. 'Hail to thee, Thane of Cawdor.' Macbeth's brow furrowed. What were the sisters saying? He was not the Thane of Cawdor! 'All hail, Macbeth,' cried the third sister, 'that shall be king hereafter!'

King? Macbeth? What kind of prophecy was this? thought Macbeth.

'And what of me?' asked Macbeth's companion.

'Hail, Banquo!' cried the first sister. 'Lesser than Macbeth, and greater.'

'Not so happy,' chimed the second, 'yet much happier.'

'Thou shalt make kings,' intoned the third, 'though thou shalt not rule.'

With that, the Weird Sisters melted into the fog, leaving the two men baffled. Were the women real, or just a dream? What was the meaning of their prophecies? The Thane of Cawdor was alive, and so was Duncan, the king!

'We must have been drugged,' said Banquo.

'Or mad, to believe that nonsense,' replied Macbeth. But the truth was, he liked what the sisters had told him. The idea of being king tempted him greatly.

Macbeth

Partner activities

I can ...

- think about the action from the point of view of one of the characters
- Write a diary entry as the character, drawing on clues from the text

1. What do you think Macbeth thought when he saw the three Weird Sisters? How did he feel when he heard what they had to say? Share ideas about this with your partner.

2. Imagine you are Macbeth. Working with your partner, write Macbeth's diary entry that night, telling about the battle and his meeting with the sisters, and his hopes for the future.

Questioning & clarifying

Imagine how things would seem from Macbeth's point of view. Keep asking yourself what he would have seen, heard, felt, etc.

Think and write

1. How did the narrator of the story come to be living on the heath?

2. Why does the narrator like to watch the Weird Sisters?

3. Which country won the battle the narrator saw in the sisters' glass?

4. What is the name of the king of Scotland?

5. Who do you think was the 'superman' whom the narrator saw in the glass?

6. Why does she describe him as a 'superman'?

7. What do the three sisters look like? Find a quote from the text that helps you work this out.

8. How does Macbeth feel when the sisters call him 'Thane of Cawdor' and 'king hereafter'? Explain why.

9. Why does Banquo think they 'must have been drugged'?

10. What kind of weather does the author describe in this text, and what effect does it have on the mood and atmosphere of the text?

Predicting

How many different types of text can you see in these three pages? From a quick look through, what do you think the text is mostly about?

FIREWORKS

The first place anyone recorded seeing fireworks was in China. It all started in the 500s, when the first firecrackers were exploded. They were just lengths of bamboo thrown onto fires – but as they heated up, the gases inside them expanded and the canes exploded with an enormous bang. Later, the explorer Marco Polo described how horses were tied up with their eyes and ears covered, to stop them from being frightened by this noise.

Proper fireworks began with the invention of gunpowder. Again, they started in China, and a whole range of fireworks was made – including rockets, sparklers and coloured flames. Western writers in the 1220s described these fireworks and started writing down 'recipes' of how to make them.

The simplest fireworks are rockets: each rocket is a tube with gunpowder packed inside it. There is a fuse into the gunpowder and a small hole in the bottom of the tube. When the fuse is lit, the powder burns. The gases made by the burning powder shoot out of the hole in the bottom and push the rocket up into the sky.

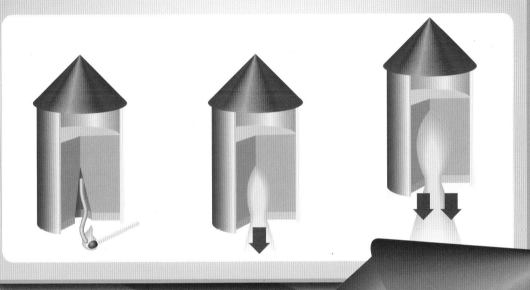

Display rockets have a second fuse which leads to more gunpowder and small fireworks, such as sparklers, coloured lights, crackers or star shells. The second fuse sets off this gunpowder when the rocket is high in the sky, to explode and spread the other fireworks around.

SETTING UP A FIREWORK DISPLAY

Have you ever wondered what goes into setting up a big fireworks display? Here are the details from Simon Page of Kimbolton Fireworks in the United Kingdom.

1

"We usually get booked about six months to a year ahead. First we visit the site. Is it in a city centre, with not much space for the fireworks to land? Are there thatched roofs or car parks nearby? We need to know, to keep the risk of fires to a minimum – then we can plan the display."

2

"It takes three to four weeks to get the fireworks ready, all packed together with their fuses ready for firing. Once they are ready, and no more than a fortnight before the display, we prepare the site."

3

"Firstly, we lay out the tubes for firing big fireworks, then lay the main cable to control the firing, and lastly we connect in all the fireworks. This can take twenty people up to ten days to do!"

KIMBOLTON FIREWORKS

4

"At last we can fire the display – twenty minutes of glory."

Fireworks

I can ...

- identify one or two aspects of a text that I think are particularly interesting
- explain to others why I think they are interesting

1. Read the text, and make a note of one or two facts or details in the text that you think are particularly interesting.

2. Explain to your partner why you thought these aspects were interesting. Does your partner agree? Together, agree on one aspect of the text that interests you both, and explain it to your teacher or to another pair.

Questioning & clarifying

As you read, keep asking yourself which facts and details are the most unusual or surprising.

Think and write

1. Name a difference between the first fireworks and fireworks now.

2. How were horses protected from early fireworks?

3. What difference did it make to fireworks when gunpowder was invented?

4. Find the diagram of a simple rocket (page 59). Write captions for the pictures in the diagram, explaining what they show.

5. What is the main difference between a simple rocket and a display rocket?

6. What does the picture at the bottom of page 58 show, and why do you think the author included it?

7. What is Simon Page's job, and what do you think he thinks of it? Find a quote that gives a clue about this.

8. Why do Simon Page's team have to visit a site before they set up a display?

9. Why might it be a problem if there were houses with thatched roofs nearby?

10. How do the team prepare the site for a display?

Questioning & clarifying

As you read, think about what the Greeks thought about their battles. Why do you think they liked to talk and write about these?

GREEK BATTLES

The Greeks loved to talk and write about their history, particularly their military exploits. They liked myths as well, usually about their gods and goddesses but sometimes stories about past battles such as the legend of the Trojan Horse.

THE STORY OF THE TROJAN HORSE

The Greeks had besieged the city of Troy in an attempt to rescue Helen, the wife of King Menelaus. She had been kidnapped by Paris, the Prince of Troy, and was also considered the most beautiful woman in the world. After ten years of fighting the Greeks were unable to break through the city's high wall, so they needed a new strategy. They built a giant, hollow wooden horse and filled it with soldiers.

Meanwhile, the rest of the Greeks went back to their ships and sailed away from Troy, which fooled the Trojans into thinking that the Greeks had given up and had left the horse as a gift. During the party the Trojans held to celebrate the 'victory', the Greeks sneaked out of the horse and opened the gates of Troy to their comrades, who had sailed back under the cover of darkness. By daylight, the Greeks had taken the whole city and won the battle.

As well as the many battles known through myths and legends, there were written accounts of actual battles, such as those between the Athenians and Spartans, and between the Greeks and the Persians. The Battle of Salamis and the Battle of Marathon are amongst the most well known.

XERXES SMASHED AT SALAMIS

Xerxes' navy surrounded

SALAMIS, 480BC

PERSIAN KING XERXES WATCHED HIS FLEET SMASHED BY THE GREEK NAVY TODAY in a decisive sea-battle just off the coast of Attica. Themistocles, the Athenian admiral, commented, "The Persians had seven hundred ships and we had just three hundred, but our smarter tactics beat the barbarians."

Themistocles went on to explain how his choice of the narrow strait between Salamis and Attica meant the Persians' bigger fleet was forced into defeat. The Persians could only get three ships at a time into the strait, and by the time they had all

IT'S AN EARLY BATH FOR THE PERSIANS

sailed in, the Greek navy was ready to strike.

Using his faster, better-crewed triremes, Themistocles surrounded Xerxes' navy with a circular 'wooden wall' of fighting ships. There was no escape for the Persians, who lost two hundred ships. Commentators now think that Xerxes will have to rethink his plans for an invasion of Greece. The Persian leader was unavailable for comment.

Xerxes, Persian leader

Greek Battles

I can ...

- read and compare two texts and sum up some of the differences
- write a new version of a text

1. Read 'The Story of the Trojan Horse' and 'Xerxes Smashed at Salamis'. Talk about the differences and similarities between the ways these texts are written. What text types are they? Which do you think is more effective, and why?

2. With your partner, rewrite 'The Story of the Trojan Horse' as a newspaper story, from the point of view of a Greek reporter. Use as many newspaper-style features as you can.

Summarising

Make notes on the main points in the story of the Trojan Horse. Then you can turn these 'facts' into newspaper-style text.

Think and write

1. In 'The Story of the Trojan Horse', what was the battle between the Greeks and Trojans about?

2. How long did the battle between Greeks and Trojans last, and why do you think it lasted so long?

3. Who won the battle of the Trojan Horse, and how?

4. Was King Menelaus Greek or Trojan? Explain how you know.

5. Why do you think the author presents the story of the Battle of Salamis as a newspaper article? Is this effective? Explain your views.

6. Which side was Themistocles on – Greek or Persian?

7. Who had more ships in the Battle of Salamis – the Greeks or the Persians?

8. Find two reasons why the Greeks beat the Persians at Salamis.

9. What is the name of the type of ship used by the Greeks?

10. Why do you think the author uses different text types for the two stories in the text? Is this effective? Why?